CRYSTAL LOVE

CRYSTAL
—LOVE—

How to Use the Earth's Magic Energy
to Fill Your Life with Love

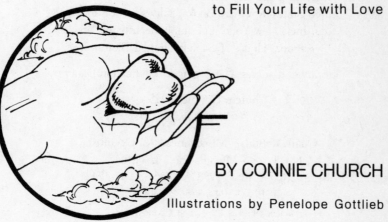

BY CONNIE CHURCH

Illustrations by Penelope Gottlieb

VILLARD BOOKS NEW YORK 1988

THIS BOOK IS DEDICATED TO

my friends, family, and loved ones whose
unconditional love and generosity of spirit have
carried me through the tough times.

All rights reserved under International and Pan-
American Copyright Conventions. Published in the
United States by Villard Books, a division of Random
House, Inc., New York, and simultaneously in Canada
by Random House of Canada Limited, Toronto.

Library of Congress Cataloging-in-Publication Data

Church, Connie, 1955–
Crystal love.

1. Quartz crystals—Miscellanea.   2. Occultism.
3. Love—Miscellanea.   I. Title.
BF1442.Q35C485   1988   133   87-27421
ISBN 0-394-75786-6 (pbk.)
BOOK DESIGN BY GUENET ABRAHAM

Manufactured in the United States of America
9 8 7 6 5 4 3 2
First edition

Thou wilt not love to live,
Unless thou live to love.
—Edmund Spenser

ACKNOWLEDGMENTS

FIRST, MY DEEP APPRECIATION TO CRYSTAL HEALER AND metaphysical psychologist Zoe Artemis, of Los Angeles and New York City, who consulted on this book. Her loving input was invaluable for making this such a special book.

As always, *endless* appreciation and thanks to my wonderful literary agent and special friend Al Lowman, Authors and Artists Group.

A very special thanks to my editor, Diane Reverand,

who never ceases to amaze me in her creativity and in her ability to "get the job done."

Also, thanks to Brian Moore, Emily Bestler, Wendy Bass, and Penelope Gottlieb for their assistance in making this book a reality.

Finally, a special thanks to Father Carroll C. Barbour for guiding me to a more profound understanding of love: "All God wants us to be are mirrors of His divine love."

CONTENTS

With this book you have received a precious gift from the earth to help fill your life with love: a rose quartz crystal. Several of the exercises in this book are intended to help you release accumulated emotional pain and trauma as you enhance your emotional well-being. However, for any persistent emotional problems, please seek professional help for the best course of additional therapy.

INTRODUCTION

WHEN RESEARCHING MY FIRST CRYSTAL BOOK, *Crystal Clear*, I discovered that the clear quartz crystal was just one of the many powerful gemstones that could be used to enhance my well-being. I was very aware of the clear quartz crystal's ability to energize, amplify, and vitalize body, mind, and spirit because of the changes that had taken place in my life while using this stone. Meditation, affirmations, and visualizations with the different clear quartz crystals I had collected were an important part of my daily routine. But until I met Zoe Artemis, a crystal healer and color therapist, I had no idea that almost every stone, from pearls to diamonds, radiates an energy that we can utilize to improve our lives.

I had my first appointment with Zoe more out of curiosity than anything else. It was hard for me to imagine exactly what a "crystal healer" did or how a crystal could "heal." Zoe works out of her home in Los Angeles, which is filled with very little furniture, but lots and lots of stones—she truly lives by what she believes in.

From the moment I entered her home I could feel a

very subtle energy coming from the many stones that fill the shelves of her living-room walls. After my first session with her I knew that I had found a real crystal healer.

A crystal healing involves a "laying on of stones"—a therapy in which the healer actually places different stones and crystals on your body, from your abdomen to the top of your head. The healer carefully picks each stone and its placement according to your physical and emotional needs. Through their color and the energy they are said to emit, it is believed that the stones can soothe and balance your energies as they are placed on the different energy centers, or chakras, that exist in every living creature. They can also amplify buried emotions and inner conflicts that may be depleting your health and sabotaging your general well-being, including your personal relationships and career goals.

During my first session with Zoe, I experienced much more than I could have ever imagined. When she finished the "layout" there were at least twenty-five stones of different shapes and colors on me. At first I felt a very pleasant tingling sensation throughout my body as she gently placed each stone. She instructed me to breathe deeply and just relax. As I did so I was aware that most of the stones had been placed on my chest, which is the center of emotion—also known as the heart chakra. Gradually, I began to feel as if I were floating and a wonderful feeling of calmness swept over me. I was in crystal bliss!

But Zoe's gentle inquiries prodded me on. They began with one simple question: "What are you feeling?"

Soon my throat began to tighten as gentle tears streamed down my face. My husband and I had recently reconciled after a very stormy period in our marriage that included a two-month separation. While we had both been at fault, I suddenly realized I was still feeling very guilty about the unhappiness I had caused him. But I had buried this emotional pain instead of dealing with it and releasing it from my being. By burying my emotions I was continuing to punish myself for something that was no longer a part of my life. I was suffering from a bad case of the guilts. Up until then, I believed that only after I had really suffered for my mistakes would I be worthy of redemption and forgiveness. It was ironic that my husband had already forgiven me and was very happy with our renewed relationship. The forgiveness I was seeking was my own. Once I could forgive myself I would be able to reconnect with my own self-love.

As Zoe guided me through this state of awareness she had me affirm: "I forgive myself. I love myself." I said this over and over as I relaxed into my deep breathing. Before the session ended, she handed me a small mirror so that I could see the crystal layout she was using.

"As you look at the layout I have created, which stone do you feel the most attracted to?"

There were six garnets dancing around my navel, amethysts on my forehead, and several stones positioned in beautiful patterns on my solar plexus, chest, and throat. It was a dazzling display fit for a princess. Of all the stones she had used, my eyes were drawn to the lush pink of the numerous rose quartz crystals that rested on my chest. They were tumbled and polished, adding beauty to their inherent soothing quality.

"This." I pointed to the large rose quartz on the center of my chest.

Zoe smiled. "I never cease to be amazed by the power of these stones. You've picked the rose quartz crystal, which is also known as the love stone. After what you have just shared with me about a part of your life that has already been resolved, it is important that you work on forgiving yourself and loving yourself. This is an area of emotional development that almost everyone needs to work on; some of us more than others, depending on the emotional traumas we have experienced during the course of our lives. The rose quartz crystal is one of the most important stones to work with because it soothes our heart and emotions as it makes us aware of the many dimensions of love. Without a happy heart, a healthy emotional state of being, we can never be at peace."

I left Zoe's house with a rose quartz crystal in my pocket, amazed by what had come up during our session. This was just the beginning of a unique therapy that was guided by the soothing energy of my rose quartz crystal. On my own and in the sessions that followed with Zoe I dealt with many aspects of my emotional state of being including unpleasant childhood memories, my relationship with my parents, and my fear of not being a good mother to my own children. Most important, I had to come to terms with the fear of my own success because over the years I had convinced myself I was unworthy of having a really good life. This was something I had never understood, but with the help of the subtle energy of my rose quartz crystal, the truth of my heart began to unfold. As the old hurts and pains began to emerge, I was finally able to deal with them and release them from my life once and for all.

The more I use my rose quartz crystal, the more uses I realize it has. My work with this stone has taken me on a profound inner journey that for the first time in my life has led to a full sense of emotional well-being. With the help of your rose quartz crystal and the love exercises in this book, you can develop emotional stability as you fill your life with love by harmonizing all the relationships in your life—beginning with yourself.

While I think that the most important function of the rose quartz crystal is to generate self-love, it is also invaluable for attracting new relationships as well as enriching existing ones with others. Through its color, pink, it radiates universal love as it arouses feelings of love, compassion, and gentleness among those who carry it and work with it. Different colors send different signals to our subconscious. The color pink sends out and attracts warmth, love, and good feelings. It has always been the color associated with love and romance, as purple has been the color associated with royalty and wisdom, and white has been the color associated with innocence.

Whereas all crystals represent the truth, the inner light that shines within all of us, the rose quartz crystal specifically represents the truth of our hearts and our capacity for love on all levels. As you work with your rose quartz crystal proceed at a pace you find comfortable. If at times you feel uneasy with the emotions you are experiencing while doing the exercises in this book, be patient and work through them. Rest assured that there is a warm, loving pink light aiding you on your journey. As guilt, jealousy, anger, and other negative emotions leave your life, the void created will be filled with love.

—Connie Church

CRYSTAL LOVE

THE ALLURE OF STONES

FOR CENTURIES MANKIND HAS BEEN HAVING A LOVE AF-
fair with gemstones of all kinds. Whether they were used
for healing, protection, self-empowerment, or adorn-
ment, the allure of precious and semiprecious stones has
enchanted numerous civilizations throughout history.
Acquiring and possessing stones, especially those in the
crystal family, has long been considered a symbol of

power. Since stones come from the earth and have existed since the beginning of creation, it once was and still is believed by many that each stone contains a part of the universal life force in the form of energy and light.

What is known about the value and importance of gemstones before the birth of Christ comes to us from legends, hieroglyphics, and artifacts found on archaeological digs. Ancient Talmudic legends depict the light source on Noah's Ark as an emormous red garnet. Proof of the therapeutic benefits of gemstones in general was recorded in a hieroglyphic papyrus, Papyrus Ebers, discovered in Egypt and dated 1500 B.C. This manuscript contains prescriptions for various ailments, including elixirs made of gemstones and minerals to facilitate cures. Over the years amulets and talismans fashioned from different gemstones, as well as goblets, shields, and breastplates inlaid with stones, have been discovered on archaeological digs all over the world.

Beyond their medicinal and more practical qualities, stones were utilized in eastern civilizations for emotional and spiritual purposes. According to their color, stones were used to strengthen character defects: Red stones were worn to curb a bad temper; blue stones to instill virtue; violet stones to restore faith; and yellow stones to relieve melancholia. Women having a difficult time conceiving wore green stones to enhance their fertility and improve their overall strength. And when it came to affairs of the heart, pink stones were worn—especially the rose quartz.

Since ancient Egypt the rose quartz has been valued as the stone of love and beauty, and was actually used as

a beauty secret. Romans and Egyptians alike believed
that rose quartz could prevent wrinkles, improve the
texture of the skin, and enhance the complexion.
Carved rose quartz facial masks have been found in
Egyptian tombs, buried with the deceased for beautifica-
tion, much in the way undertakers today use makeup or
special clothes.

Egyptian women believed that wearing rose quartz
jewelry made them more desirable and helped attract
love into their lives. Both bride and groom in ancient
Egyptian marriage ceremonies wore a pouch around their
necks or their waists filled with pieces of rose quartz—a
symbol of their eternal love for each other. Even then
the rose quartz was used to send love, attract love, and
harmonize personal relationships. When working on
spiritual development, the rose quartz was carried to
symbolize kindness, compassion, and understanding. It
was and still is considered the *love stone*.

STONE POWER TODAY

While civilizations have come and gone, our romance
with the stone has persevered. While stone lore has
always been practiced on some level, gemstones have
been collected primarily for their monetary and aesthetic
value in the twentieth century. Now the power of quartz
crystals, in particular, is upon us as we rediscover the
belief in their transformational properties and apply
these beliefs to our modern times.

The precision of the crystal's vibrating energy field has

made radio, satellite communications, telephone, and television possible. Laser surgery and computer technology both utilize, in their precision and high-tech capabilities, crystal power.

When squeezed and released, or rubbed in the palm of your hand, quartz crystals produce small electrical charges that vibrate within a positive and negative energy field. What was once considered to be a "magical quality" in these stones may simply be the laws of nature and energy functioning. However, combine the energy of quartz crystals with your own electromagnetic field and mental abilities, and watch the magic begin!

If you have been working with a clear quartz crystal, you are probably aware of its capacity for transmitting, amplifying, and focusing your energy. It is the perfect tool for personal transformation as it helps to create your thoughts, emotions, and desires into reality.

While the rose quartz crystal is equally powerful in its own way, it has a more subtle and profound energy. You won't feel that same tingle of energy that you often feel when you hold a clear quartz in your hand—but rest assured that its very subtle energy is working, smoothing and soothing emotions.

The rose quartz is also an important tool for personal transformation, specifically on an emotional level as it helps to bring about emotional balance, renewal, and development. The eighties has become a decade for growth, awareness, self-help, and personal truth, and the rose quartz crystal is one of the most important stones you can use to find true happiness, as it helps you learn what love really is.

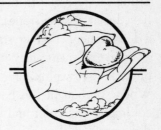

CRYSTALS FIRST BEGAN FORMING ABOUT TWO HUNDRED million years ago in quartz veins that run through sandstone deposits within the earth. They begin to grow when water and sand combine under very intense temperature, pressure, and energy conditions.

Whereas the clear quartz crystal grows in a crystalline form, the rose quartz forms as massive rock. When it is mined, it is often dynamited and brought out in large twenty- or thirty-pound chunks. It is then crushed and strained according to size specifications. Although it is not necessary, pieces are often tumbled and polished like yours. Many crystal users believe that tumbling and polishing the rose quartz increases its energy. It is also believed that opaque stones, like your rose quartz, radiate a denser energy than crystalline or transparent stones.

Your rose quartz may be milky white with a hint of pink, deep rosy pink, or a shade somewhere in between. When you bought this book you probably picked it according to the color and shape of the crystal you liked the best. You also selected your crystal for the energy it vibrates, as it is mutually attracted to your energy. While it may be hard to believe, there is a special energy connection between you and your rose quartz crystal. This is what makes your rose quartz such an important love tool for the changes you want to bring about in your emotional life.

If this book and rose quartz were given to you as a gift, think of it as a love gift. And even as a gift, an energy connection was made between you and your rose quartz, because whoever purchased this book for you probably picked it according to the stone they thought you would like the best.

Before you begin using your rose quartz, or love stone, there are some simple crystal rituals you should follow. These little rituals are important for crystal care and will help you tune in to the power of your love stone so that you can realize its full potential.

CARING FOR YOUR LOVE STONE

You'll want to remove any energy patterns or vibrations your love stone may have absorbed before it came to you. It's important to do this before you begin carrying your love stone with you or using it in any of the love exercises in this book. This is done by manually and mentally clearing it. While there are many methods you can use, I recommend this simple clearing technique that uses running tap water and some easy visualizations:

- • • In your right hand, hold your love stone between your thumb and index finger. Turn on the faucet and allow the cool tap water to bathe it for about one minute.

- • • Imagine that the water is running through your love stone as well as over it, washing it clean of any energy it absorbed on its journey to you. Imagine that as the old energy washes out of your love stone, it goes down the drain and is diluted into nothingness. This process only takes a minute but you may continue it longer, until you feel that your love stone is absolutely clean and clear.

For a once-a-week super cleaning and clearing, give your love stone a salt bath. There are two ways to do this. You can:

- • • Mix a teaspoon of salt into one cup of water and allow your stone to soak from ten minutes to seven

days. (For large volume, mix half a pound of sea salt into one gallon of water.) After a salt bath always rinse your stone with running tap water, or

• • • Bury your crystal in a cup of sea salt for three hours to seven days. Again, always rinse your stone with running tap water.

In both methods the amount of time involved is up to you. Make your decision according to *how you feel.* Some crystal users feel that the minimal amount of time for either method is adequate.

Besides the initial cleaning and clearing, it's a good idea to repeat this process after you have done any of the exercises that involve a negative energy release.

All crystals thrive on light, so an occasional sun bath will stimulate the natural flow of your love stone's energy. Place it on a windowsill, porch, terrace, or anywhere that it can receive direct sunlight for about ten minutes a day. The sun will give your love stone a super charge from noon until two P.M.

Your love stone will also benefit from moonlight. Just as the different phases of the moon affects our emotions, they will also enhance the energy of the love stone.

CONNECTING WITH YOUR LOVE STONE

After you have cleaned, cleared, and charged your love stone, rub it with a soft cloth to restore its luster. Focus

on its color. Perhaps it's milky white with a few strips of pink in it, or maybe it's rosy pink with a hint of white on the end. Its smooth, polished roundness feels wonderful when you rub it with your thumb while holding it in the palm of your hand. I know an Episcopal priest who prays and meditates while holding his love stone. He says that he finds the feel of it comforting, that it is the perfect "rubbing stone," easing worry and uneasiness.

During the first few days that you have your love stone, it's best if you do nothing more than sit quietly with it for about ten minutes a day. At this time your vibrations will begin to merge with its vibrations. This simple exercise will help you attune yourself to your love stone's energy:

The Love Stone Connection

• • • Sit quietly in a peaceful environment, holding your love stone in your left hand against your heart.

• • • Breathe deeply, inhaling and exhaling 6-8 counts, as you calm yourself mentally and physically.

• • • Now imagine that you are breathing in a loving, warm, pink light.

• • • Imagine that you are filling up with this pink light. Feel its gentleness. Let its soothing energy become a part of you.

• • • Stay with this feeling, breathing deeply. Sit for a few moments before getting up.

You'll also want to keep your love stone with you at all times for the first thirty days you have it. It's a good idea to carry it in a small pouch or bag made of natural fibers. Or you can wrap it in a small piece of cloth. This will protect it from loose change and other objects in your pocket or purse.

During this period take your love stone to bed with you. Tuck it under your pillow or sleep with it in your hand. Because of its smoothness and easy shape, you'll probably still be holding it when you wake up.

Keep it with you when you bathe or shower. This is an excellent time to clean and clear it. You can hold it under the running water with you, as you imagine any accumulated negative energy washing off and out of both of you.

After this thirty-day period it is no longer necessary to sleep or bathe with your love stone, as your energies will have merged. But keep this stone with you wherever you go. Your love stone is the perfect companion, reinforcing your self-love and bolstering your confidence at all times. Also, you never know when you are going to want to attract or send love!

SHARING YOUR LOVE STONE WITH OTHERS

Of all the crystals you can work with the love stone is the most personal, as it amplifies your feelings and emotional vulnerabilities. Therefore, I think it is important that you keep your love stone to yourself.

After you have worked with your love stone, its energy is merged with yours and it is basically in sync with your emotional patterns. Allowing someone else to handle it could confuse the energy. If a friend or relative is in need of a love stone, it's best if you buy him his own rather than allowing him to share yours. And as I said before, a love stone is the perfect gift for someone you care about.

If, accidentally, someone else handles your love stone, clean it, clear it, and merge with it again by repeating the Love Stone Connection exercise.

AWARENESS TECHNIQUES

Now that you are familiar with the crystal rituals, there are some basic awareness techniques you need to understand that will provide a foundation for many of the exercises in this book. These awareness techniques include: *listening to your inner voice, deep breathing, visualizing your heart's desire,* and *affirming to reinforce.* All of these techniques will help you connect with your inner self, a necessary connection for enhancing your emotional life.

Listening to Your Inner Voice

Your inner voice can be defined in several ways. You may think of it as your intuition, your gut feeling, or what you always thought to be your sixth sense. It may appear to you as a verbal response that only you can hear (a little voice in your head) or as a simple mental picture. Or your inner voice may be nothing more than an intuitive feeling that comes over you from time to time.

As you work with your love stone you will become very aware of your inner voice. As it amplifies your emotions, your deepest feelings will begin to emerge. Don't be afraid of what you're hearing. Listening to it and accepting it is an important part of your emotional development. Trust what you hear and consider it carefully as you chart your emotional course.

Your inner voice usually shares with you your real feelings, as it expresses your subconscious mind. While you might not always like what you hear, know that it can help provide solutions to your personal problems and resolutions to your emotional conflicts.

Deep Breathing

When working with your love stone your energy should be calm, centered, and focused so that you are relaxed. One of the best ways to relax is through gentle deep breathing. This allows you to tune in to your inner voice and connect with your deepest emotions.

This deep breathing technique can be used whenever you are feeling tense or stressed out; it is a natural relaxant. While your body position will change depending on the exercise, use this deep breathing technique throughout the book whenever you are told to "begin your deep breathing" or "breathe deeply."

• • • Sit in a comfortable chair with your back straight, shoulders down, feet flat on the floor, and your arms resting comfortably at your side. Do nothing more for a minute, making sure you are comfortable and adjusting your position if you're not.

• • • Now place your hands on your abdomen. Slowly inhale through your nose to the count of 1–2–3–4–5–6–7–8. Feel your breath move through your chest into your stomach, and finally into your abdomen. If you are a shallow breather, at first you may be more comfortable inhaling to the count of 6 rather than 8. After some practice you will be able to comfortably inhale the full 8 counts.

• • • Slowly exhale to the count of 1–2–3–4–5–6–7–8. Again, you may be more comfortable exhaling to the count of 6, working up to 8 counts after some practice.

• • • As you deeply inhale and exhale imagine your breath with your eyes, hear it through your ears, and feel it move throughout your body. Become nothing more than the breath, being at one with the moment.

• • • Repeat the entire process five times, as you feel yourself flow into a deep sense of relaxation.

Visualizing Your Heart's Desire

Creative visualization is the process of consciously using your will and imagination to create what you want in your life. When you visualize, you create a clear mental picture of events, people, places, and things that you would like to have in your life. Visualization can best be defined as specific thoughts that have an intention.

Through visualization and the power of your mind, you can structure your thoughts in such a way that they become a reality. The power of visualization is based on the principle that ideas precede form, or that thoughts are things. By taking a desire and turning it into a full-blown mental picture that you repeatedly imagine in your mind, your fully visualized desire can manifest and become that reality.

When you first begin visualizing you may be able to only "think" about what you desire. With practice, as the energy of your love stone amplifies your visualizations, you will begin to "see" clearly what you desire. The more details you add to your visualizations, the more real they appear and the more powerful they become.

There are two types of visualization to use when working with your love stone: active and passive. When you visualize actively you create detailed mental pictures, and then send those pictures out into the universe so that they can become a reality. As you visualize you also program your subconscious mind, so that your actions support your visualizations. Your love stone helps to empower your actions, as it gives you that boost of confidence to take the next step forward.

Through passive visualization and with the help of your love stone, you will be interpreting and dealing with the different thoughts and feelings that come up while you are in a state of deep relaxation. Passive visualization will help you process the old hurts and remove your emotional stumbling blocks as you release any negative energy you are currently experiencing or that has accumulated over the years.

For instance, if you are working on creating a better relationship with your parents, passive visualization will expose painful childhood experiences that still linger in your heart. Once they emerge, you will be able to release them. This will help ease present conflicts you have with your parents.

Affirming to Reinforce

Reinforcing your visualizations with strong, positive affirmations will strengthen your intentions and desire. To affirm your desire means to "make firm" what you want to draw in to your life, as you state *what is*—as though it is already happening. The word "affirm" is the root word of affirmative, which means yes.

Whether your affirmations are verbal, written, or said to yourself, it is important that they are simply structured and always constructed in the present tense. For

instance, if you are looking for a new romantic relationship you would affirm:

"I have a lover who is perfect for me"
not
"I will find a new lover who is perfect for me."

When you affirm, really feel and believe that what
you are affirming is happening at that moment. The
stronger your affirmations, the more they enhance and
provide a solid foundation for your visualizations.

If you have trouble really feeling and believing what
you are affirming, set aside some quiet time every day to
write out your affirmations. Eventually, your doubts will
vanish and you will begin to believe what you are affirming. Never doubt the potential of your visualizations and
affirmations.

RECEIVING AND SENDING LOVE

When working with your love stone keep in mind that
energy flows in the left hand and out the right hand.
Your left hand receives the love energy you attract
through your love stone, while your right hand sends
your love energy out into the universe through your love
stone. So if you are hoping to receive love or are visualizing or affirming your heart's desires, hold your love
stone in your left hand. When sending out unconditional love or projecting your desire into action, hold
your love stone in your right hand.

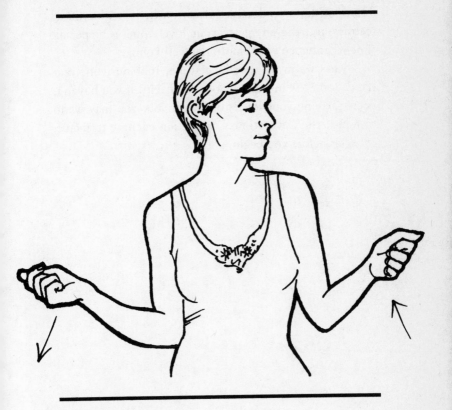

GETTING STARTED

Before you begin any exercise in this book read through
it a few times to become familiar with it. This will help
the process flow. The more you work with these exercises, the more effective they will be. You'll also want to
perform them in a peaceful environment, alone. This
means no telephone calls or interruptions of any kind.

Think of this well-deserved respite with your innermost feelings and the energy of your love stone as a special time to enhance your emotional well-being.

Always warm up your love stone, rubbing it in your hand, for a few minutes before you begin. If you haven't been carrying your love stone with you, you may want to repeat the Love Stone Connection exercise to merge energies before you begin.

YOUR LOVE STONE AND YOUR ◆ 3
EMOTIONAL WELL-BEING

YOUR LOVE STONE IS YOUR SPECIAL LOVE TALISMAN. JUST
by carrying it with you, occasionally holding it in your
hand and gazing into its beautiful pink glow, you will
begin to notice subtle changes occurring within you.
You will be more aware of your emotions and more sensitive to the feelings of others. As you become emotionally centered, your self-esteem will improve and your
thoughts will become more loving in general. Rather
than automatically thinking the worst of someone or

something, until you are proven wrong, you will probably give new people and new situations the benefit of the doubt—even thinking the best about them. With the help of your love stone, compassion, understanding, and harmony will create the foundation of your daily routines.

Your loving approach to life will intensify as you let your love stone become your love tool. With the help of the different love exercises in this book, as the subtle energies of your love stone soothe and balance your chakras, you will develop an awareness and connectedness with your own emotional self that can help to harmonize all the relationships in your life.

WHAT ARE THE CHAKRAS?

Within your body there are seven major energy points, or chakras, where your vital life force is increased and your energy is focused. Each chakra has its own characteristics, according to where it's located and the gland, color, and level of human behavior it corresponds to. It is believed that together these seven chakras create your energy system as they keep the vital life force moving throughout your body. The following chart and diagram will provide you with a general overview of the chakra system.

The correlation of the chakras to our total well-being was first realized in early civilizations by healers and seers, who observed these energy points as spinning

This Chakra	At This Location	Vibrates This Color	And Corresponds To
1st	Pubic Bone	Red	Your Activity Level (Energy, Motivation, Sexuality)
2nd	Navel Area	Orange	Courage/Confidence
3rd	Solar Plexus	Yellow	Career/Business
4th	Chest	Pink/ Green	Relationships
5th	Throat	Blue	Communication
6th	Third Eye (above nose, between brows)	Violet	Intuition/ Subconscious Mind
7th	Crown (top of head)	White	Enlightenment/ Spirituality

wheels. The term "chakra" literally means "wheel" in Sanskrit. These healers and seers found that when the body was free of tension, stress, and emotional pain the life force flowed freely and good health was maintained. Poor health and disease often followed when one or more of these points became blocked. This ancient concept, well documented in numerous ancient Yogic and Tantric texts, has persisted through the ages and is being actively explored today as we investigate alternative methods of healing and what we can do to help ourselves.

It is believed that the different people, situations, and things you attract into your life are determined by your level of consciousness, or the chakra from which you are operating. If any of these people, situations, or things

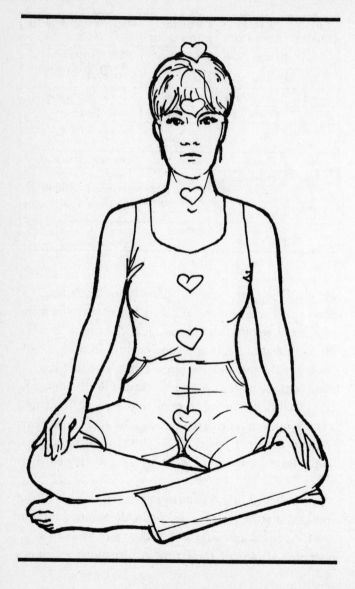

create negative or unpleasant experiences, the corresponding chakra may become blocked. Unless it is confronted and released, the emotional pain associated with these negative experiences remain within your body, ultimately creating an energy imbalance. Once this imbalance occurs, the corresponding gland is affected, leading to a breakdown of the physical body. This is why maintaining chakra balance is so important for your total well-being.

While each chakra is important and contributes equally to your well-being, everything radiates from the heart chakra, your emotional center. For it is how you feel at any given moment and how you assimilate your feelings that affects every aspect of your life and influences the energy flow of all the other chakras.

YOUR LOVE CENTER

Your heart chakra is the focus of your entire being as it is the point of centeredness and balance. Think of it as your love center, encompassing every aspect of love, for it is here that all your emotional experiences are processed and stored. Unless you constantly confront and release your emotional pain, your heart chakra becomes blocked from too many emotional burdens. This makes it difficult for you to love and be loved.

Your love stone's energy gently penetrates your heart chakra, amplifying suppressed and unresolved traumas, emotions, and insecurities that often originate in child-

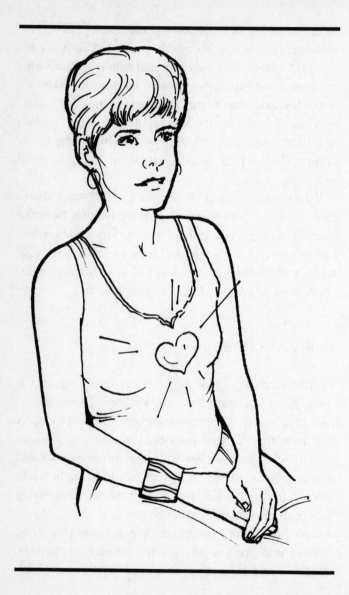

hood. As all your feelings begin to surface, your love stone soothes your emotions and helps you release any negativity associated with them. By letting go of your emotional burdens, the love flow is restored and brings with it a sense of emotional well-being.

YOUR EMOTIONAL TUNE-UP

One of the best ways to maintain your emotional well-being is to give yourself an emotional tune-up. This involves laying your love stone on each one of your chakras. When this is done your chakra system is at once stimulated and soothed by the energy of your love stone. As you place your love stone on each chakra it channels soothing pink light into the body, bringing to focus any negative emotions you're feeling as they identify with that chakra. Once they emerge, you can release them with the help of your visualizations and affirmations.

You should give yourself an emotional tune-up once a week. If this is done consistently, you will develop a connection with your inner self that will help remove any emotional blocks and enable you to become a flowing channel of love. You should allow at least twenty minutes for this two-part process, and perform it in a part of your home where you feel the most emotionally comfortable and secure.

Before you begin your emotional tune-up, study the following chart. It will give you a better understanding of the emotions that are identified with each chakra.

This Chakra	Corresponds to These Negative Emotions
1st	impatience, anger, violence, manipulation, sexual obsession, revenge
2nd	sluggishness, pomposity, cruelty, lack of emotional warmth, materialism
3rd	laziness, cowardice, cynicism, choosiness, criticism
4th	jealousy, possessiveness, insecurity, envy, self-loathing
5th	depression, isolation, inability to communicate, fixedness and inability to accept change
6th	superstition, fear, inability to live in the moment
7th	arrogance, conceit, power hunger, need to control

Part One

• • • Lie down on a comfortable flat surface and bend your knees so that your lower back feels relaxed.

• • • Place your love stone on your heart chakra, the center of your chest. Now begin your deep breathing.

• • • For a few minutes do nothing more than your deep breathing, allowing your body to completely relax. Remember that it's a slow 6–8 counts in, and a slow 6–8 counts out.

• • • As you inhale deeply, imagine that you are breathing in a warm pink light. As you exhale deeply, feel any accumulated tension leave your body. Continue doing this until you feel that your body

is completely filled with wonderful, warm, loving, pink light.

• • • Now spend some time reviewing the different areas in your life: your relationship with your lover or spouse, friendships, parents, children, your job. Consider the following questions:

In the past week, how did things go in each of these areas?

Were there any disagreements or fights?

Was anything said or done to you that hurt your feelings?

Did you do or say anything that hurt someone else's feelings?

• • • Look deeply within yourself, analyzing honestly what went on. After you've gone through your week, try to decide the primary negative emotion you felt or negative quality you exhibited. For instance, did you feel a lot of jealousy, insecurity, or anger? Perhaps you were critical, cynical, or arrogant. Allow yourself to relive your feelings. And if you feel like crying, let the tears flow. Crying is a healthy release.

• • • Once you have pinpointed this emotion or quality, release it with the following affirmations:

"I release my: (*jealousy, anger, resentment, possessiveness, laziness, etc.*)
"I love myself. I forgive myself."

• • • Let your deep breathing enhance your affirmation. As you inhale, feel yourself filling up with a loving pink light. On the exhale affirm out loud or silently: "I release my _____. I love myself. I forgive myself."

• • • Continue with your pink light inhalation and affirming exhalation at least ten times, or until you begin to "believe your words."

• • • Now finish by saying, "So it is."

• • • Continue to relax into your deep breathing for a few minutes before you begin part two.

Part Two

• • • Depending on the primary negative emotion or quality that surfaced in part one, place your love stone on the corresponding chakra. (You'll want to refer to the chart until you become familiar with the chakras and the corresponding emotions.)

• • • As an example I'll use "criticism," which corresponds to the third chakra.

• • • With your love stone on your third chakra, *recreate the scene as you remember it.* (I criticized my husband for not spending enough time with the children. Given that he is working ten hours a day, it's not surprising that he's exhausted by the time he comes home. Instead of simply expressing

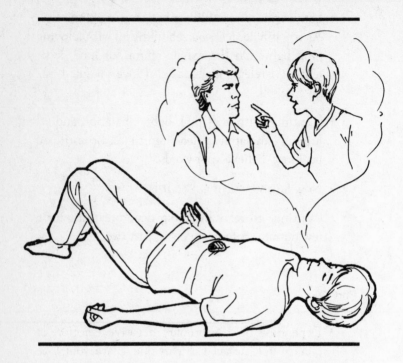

how I feel, I continue to criticize other aspects of his life; that he spends too many Saturdays on the golf course, etc. My husband becomes angry, storms into our bedroom, slamming the door behind him. We don't speak until the following evening.)

• • • After you have re-created the scene as vividly as possible, confront yourself. Take responsibility for your part of the conflict.

• • • Now enclose the scene, the conflict, and negative

emotions associated with it in a pink bubble. See
the pink bubble floating off into the distance, becoming smaller and smaller, out of your life for-
ever. As you watch it float away begin affirming
out loud or silently: "I love myself. I forgive myself."

• • • Again, allow your deep breathing to enhance your
affirmation.

After your weekly tune-up, do something special for
yourself. Have a massage, take a bubble bath, or buy
that new novel you've been wanting to read. Maybe an
evening out with a loved one or close friend. The point
is to treat yourself to something special to reinforce that
you do "love yourself and forgive yourself," and that you
are deserving of the good things in life.

THE POWER OF
UNCONDITIONAL LOVE

WHEN YOUR LIFE IS GOING SMOOTHLY IT IS USUALLY BE-cause you're satisfied with your job, your children are happy and healthy, and you're relating well with your friends, family, and spouse or lover. At this time in your life it's easier to be loving to, tolerant and understanding of those who are less fortunate. There's room in your heart for the homeless on the street or the child who comes to your door selling raffle tickets, so that he can earn a new bike or a special trip. At times like this you can spare a few extra dollars and a warm smile.

But the real test of our capacity to love is when your life is filled with problems and more negative emotions than you know how to handle. For to love truly is to love unconditionally—to love "no matter what."

How do you smile and continue to send out loving thoughts and positive energy when you feel as if your heart is about to break, or when you feel overwhelmed with bitterness, jealousy, or anger? Simply by presenting a positive emotional tone and applying the principle of unconditional love. No matter how bleak your life may seem, regardless of the emotional pain someone may have caused you, if you can get beyond your emotions at that moment, keep a smile on your face, and send out unconditional love, it will come back to you in a wonderful way.

Your love stone can help empower your visualizations and affirmations of unconditional love by amplifying and sending your loving feelings out into the universe. The feelings you send out have a specific energy or vibration that attracts and draws back into your life a like energy or vibration. So the more love you send out, unconditional and from the heart, the more that love will come back to fill your life. Working with unconditional love is one of the simplest but most powerful methods you have to fill your life with love.

PROGRAMMING YOUR LOVE STONE DAILY WITH YOUR UNCONDITIONAL LOVE

Begin each day in a loving way, regardless of how you feel, by programming your love stone with your unconditional love. After you've done this you'll want to carry your stone with you throughout the day, holding it and focusing on it from time to time to remind you of the unconditional love you've beamed out into the universe.

- • • Before you leave for work or begin your daily routine, sit comfortably in a chair or on a pillow on the floor.

- • • With your love stone in your right hand, held next to your heart, begin your deep breathing. As you inhale, imagine a vibrant pink light filling you up.

- • • Begin to see in your mind's eye the different people you will be encountering or working with during your day. With a smile on your face send loving thoughts to all of these people, whether it's your co-workers at the office or the cashier at the grocery store. As you exhale, imagine your love as a vibrant beam of pink light going from your heart through your love stone and into their hearts.

- • • Now see in your mind's eye anyone you are having a conflict with or whom you don't particularly like. This could be anyone in your life—mother-in-law, sister, friend, spouse, or boss. Regardless

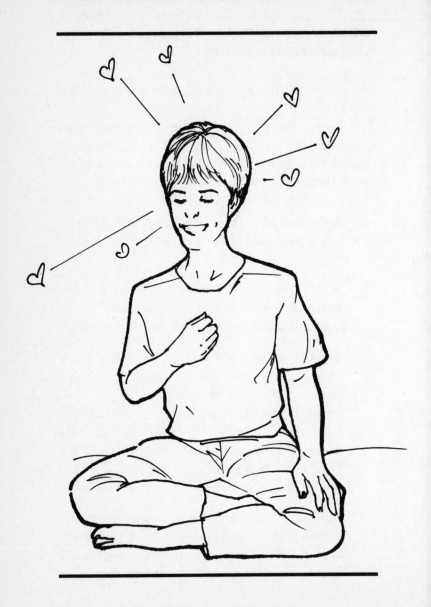

of any anger or unhappiness you feel toward them, forgive them and let it go as you exhale. You may want to reinforce this by affirming: "I forgive ＿＿ for all hurts, both real and imagined."

• • • Repeat this as many times as you feel is necessary.

• • • Now inhale deeply the vibrant pink light, and as you exhale send them your love as a vibrant pink light going from your heart through your love stone and into their hearts. While you may experience some resistance, continue doing this until you really feel you are sending them your unconditional love. These are the people who really need it.

• • • Sit quietly for a few moments as you see yourself feeling loved, secure, and joyful throughout your day.

• • • Now take your love stone from your heart and hold it up to your third eye—above the nose and between your brows—and affirm out loud or silently: "You are filled with my unconditional love as you guide me through my day." Repeat this seven times. Know, feel, and believe that your love stone is your love tool.

As you go through your day, if any feelings of negativity about someone else suddenly pop up or you find yourself caught in a conflict, rub your love stone in your hand as

you again silently affirm: "You are filled with my unconditional love as you guide me through my day."

■ ■ ■

Program your love stone with your unconditional love
every day. Make it your morning ritual before you leave
your house. Be confident in knowing that your love
stone is "on alert," ready to reaffirm your unconditional
love. With the power of your love stone, regardless of
anyone else's actions or words, when you love unconditionally your relationships will improve because the love
energy you send out touches the hearts of everyone in
your life.

BEFORE YOU CAN HAVE A HAPPY, SATISFYING, AND FUL-
filling relationship with someone else, whether it be
lover, spouse, child, parent, sibling or friend, you must
develop self-love. When you have self-love you connect
with your inner truth and accept yourself as that truth
—for this is who you are. This doesn't mean that you
shouldn't continue to change, grow, and become a better person. What it does mean is that you love yourself
"no matter what." Think of self-love as your uncondi-

tional love turned inward; the trick is to believe that you deserve it! If others deserve your unconditional love, why not you too?

Since your first real relationship begins with yourself, how you feel about yourself is reflected in your approach to all of your other relationships. For instance, if you feel unworthy of love you may pick a lover or spouse who physically or verbally abuses you. Instead of ending this destructive relationship, you might just maintain it because you believe it is what you deserve.

The energy you project out into the world is rooted in how you feel about yourself. That energy determines the quality of relationships you attract into your life. This is why developing your self-love is so important. Self-love is your stepping stone to all of your other relationships.

UNDERSTANDING YOUR INNER CHILD

I wonder if it is possible for any of us to ever receive as much love as we feel we need. Unfortunately, when we don't feel that we're getting enough love we begin to doubt our self-worth and diminish our self-love. While every personal circumstance is unique, it's important to remember that we are all in this together, that we must all look deep within ourselves and work on developing and strengthening our self-love. Even if you feel emotionally intact right now and terrific about who you are, it is still important that you nurture your self-love for your continual emotional growth and for the times in your life when you may have no one to depend on but you.

A lack of love perceived during your childhood could be the source of any low self-esteem or lack of self-worth and self-love you currently feel. The unraveling of the self-love you were born with might have begun innocently—the first time you didn't get that hug or kiss you needed. While your parents might have loved you to the best of their ability, chances are good that you just weren't nurtured or loved enough or in the exact way that you needed to be loved. There are many other variables as well: Perhaps you grew up in a broken home, divided between the love of both parents. Maybe you lost a parent or were reared by an alcoholic.

As you grew up, the little hurts, traumas, and painful memories left their imprint, undermining your self-image. But you have the power to create your self-love and repair the emotional damage that might have occurred. Regardless of what transpired in the past, you must reconnect with the self-love you born with so that you feel worthy of love and are able to attract quality love into your life.

Loving Your Inner Child

In order to reconnect with the self-love you were born with, as well as strengthen the self-love you already feel, you need to step back in time and reacquaint yourself with your inner child. Your inner child is that little

person who is the keeper of your heart, holding on to all of the hurts of your past, holding you back from your self-love.

The following exercise empowers you to be the parent your inner child always needed. When combined with the soothing energy of your love stone, this exercise helps you care for, love, and nurture your inner child as you develop self-love.

• • • Find a comfortable place to sit and hold your love stone in your left hand. Begin your deep breathing to relax, to center yourself, and to clear your mind.

• • • Imagine that you are sitting on a beach, feeling peaceful and serene as you watch and listen to the tide flow in and out. Smell the ocean. Continue with this for a couple of minutes, and project all of these thoughts into your love stone.

• • • As you look down the beach see a child walking toward you. As this little boy or girl approaches you, see that it is you when you were five years old. Embrace your inner child as you gaze into your own five-year-old eyes with tenderness and love.

• • • Feel that your inner child is thrilled to be with you. Let your inner child know how much you love and need him or her. Reassure your inner child that you'll always be there, no matter what.

• • • Feel the love in your heart for your inner child and project it into your love stone. Create a loving pink energy field around the two of you.

• • • Focus on the love and warmth you are feeling as you are reunited with your inner child. Continue your deep breathing and then after a few minutes open your eyes. Know that you have made peace with your inner child.

As you repeat this exercise consistently at least a couple of times a week, you will be amazed by the relationship you develop with your inner child as you begin to love, honor, and respect yourself.

You can develop this exercise further by creating a dialogue with your inner child. Whenever you see, feel, or hear something that makes you happy, angry, or sad, silently ask your inner child how he or she feels about it. Allow your inner child to answer you. You will be amazed and delighted by the responses you receive.

This dialogue will provide clues to how you really feel about the different situations and problems that are a part of your life. The truth of your heart will emerge, making it impossible to deny your true feelings, feelings that you need to express and act on.

Take the time and make the effort to maintain this silent, ongoing dialogue with your inner child. This is your opportunity to love, nurture, and support a part of yourself that has felt neglected since you were a child.

COPING WITH SADNESS

When you learn to love your inner child, you become more emotionally connected. As your heart opens up your emotions evolve and your level of awareness soars. This means that the "good times" become the "best times," as you are more sensitive to all of your emotional moments.

We all want, work for, and relish the happy moments. But regardless of the amount of happiness and the abundance of love you attract into your life, in all probability there will still be periods of sadness with which you must cope. For instance: a sudden change in life-style, losing a job, the death of a loved one, or dealing with the end of an important relationship—these are all common life experiences that can cause sadness and corresponding feelings of loneliness, hopelessness, despair, and depression. If left unchecked, these feelings can turn into emotional handicaps that deplete self-love.

While you don't want to perpetuate it, one of the worst ways to deal with your sadness is to deny it. If you do, your unresolved feelings will become buried in your heart and block your love flow. You need to accept that sadness as your reality at that moment, confront and embrace it, and then ultimately release it.

The following exercise can help ease you through periods of sadness or times when you feel you are in a state of emotional crisis. Remember, your love stone is first and foremost your heart soother helping you to maintain your emotional balance.

• • • Lie down on a comfortable flat surface and bend your knees so that your lower back feels relaxed.

• • • Place your love stone on your heart chakra, the center of your chest. Begin your deep breathing and allow your body to completely relax.

• • • As you inhale deeply, imagine that you are breathing in a warm pink light. As you exhale deeply, feel the tension leave your body.

• • • Once you feel relaxed, specify your sadness. For instance, is it:

—loneliness?

—hopelessness?

—despair?

—depression?

• • • Now vividly re-create in your mind the events that brought forth your emotion. It is important that you really confront and play out in your mind what has happened.

• • • Check your breathing. If it has become shallow, focus on breathing deeply. If you feel like crying, let it all out. You must face your emotions before you can release them.

• • • Now enclose all of your sadness and all of the images that come to mind in a pink bubble.

• • • Deeply inhale the soothing pink light, and on each exhale imagine that you are blowing the bubble farther and farther away, until it is gone. See, know, and feel that your sadness is drifting away into the past.

• • • Take a few minutes to just breathe deeply and calm yourself.

• • • Finish by affirming on each exhale: "My (*loneliness*) is gone." Repeat this affirmation as many times as you desire. Hear, know, and feel that your sadness is gone.

• • • Rest for a few minutes before getting up.

Repeat this exercise daily until your sadness or emotional crisis has passed. Keep your love stone with you at all times, reaffirming as often as possible "My (*loneliness*) is gone."

You should also consider what activities you can add to your daily routine or changes you can make to help push you over the hump so that you can get on with your life. But don't be too demanding or hard on yourself during these vulnerable periods. In fact, think of ways to pamper yourself as a reward for having the courage to confront and deal with your feelings. It's a healthy sign of self-love when you take action to restore and maintain your emotional balance.

GUILT: THE SELF-LOVE SABOTAGE

Guilt is the ultimate self-love sabotage, making you feel that you don't deserve to be loved or successful. It is the illusion that you must suffer, and suffer hard, for the mistakes you have made before you are worthy of redemption and forgiveness.

Guilt is a form of self-punishment that nobody deserves. It does not heal, and if left unchecked can lead us on a course of self-destruction. Often alcoholism, drug abuse, and many emotional problems stem from unresolved feelings of guilt.

Making Amends

If you are to be a healthy, happy, loving person then you must realize and accept that guilt has no place in your life. When you make a mistake, instead of feeling guilty, deal with it immediately by making amends to the person(s) you have hurt.

• • • Sit comfortably, holding your love stone in your right hand. Begin your deep breathing to center and calm yourself.

• • • Now begin to analyze and evaluate the mistake you made. Ask yourself the following questions:

—Whom did I hurt?

—How did I hurt them?

—What was my motivation?

—What have I learned from this mistake, and what can I do to keep from repeating it?

• • • Now hold your love stone to your third eye—
between the brows and above your nose—and ask
yourself this final question:

—What can I do to make amends to the person(s) I
hurt or what can I do to correct my mistake?

• • • Listen to your inner voice. It will guide you.

Perhaps a telephone call and an apology are all that are
necessary. Or maybe it's best for you to sit down and
write a letter. Whatever method you choose, don't try
to justify or defend your mistake. Just humbly apologize.
After you have made your amends, hold your love stone
in your left hand and affirm: "I forgive myself for the
mistakes I have made."

If your mistake has gone unnoticed but you are feeling
guilty anyway, go out of your way to do something nice
for the person(s) involved. Offer them a ride home from
work, take them out to lunch, offer to help them with a
project they're involved with, or buy them a crystal—
they'll think you're terrific and you'll feel good about
yourself because you've amended your mistake.

Making Amends for Past Mistakes

• • • With pad and pencil in hand sit comfortably,
begin your deep breathing, and hold your love

stone in the opposite hand you write with. Take a few moments to center yourself and clear your mind.

• • • Think about the different people in your life whom you have hurt in some way over the years. Write their names down. While this list could go back ten years or more, don't force this process; only be concerned with the names and events that float freely into your mind. What you have forgotten you no longer feel guilty about.

• • • Review your list. As you see each person in your mind affirm: "I am sorry for my mistake—the hurt and the pain."

• • • Now hold your rose quartz in your right hand, next to your heart, and beam loving pink light from your heart through your love stone and into their heart.

• • • Exhale deeply and release your guilt into the past, where it belongs.

• • • Repeat this process with every person on your list.

Your Guilt Release Affirmation

While you're working on releasing any accumulated guilt, affirm as often as possible: "I deserve happiness and to have my needs met."

You can affirm this silently or out loud when you're

on your way to work, shop, run errands, or when you're cooking, cleaning, or exercising. Remember, the more often you affirm, the more powerful the affirmation becomes.

PROGRAMMING SELF-LOVE

Regardless of how you have felt about yourself in the past or how you feel about yourself right now, you can let go of your negative self-image and replace it with a positive self-image by programming self-love. The following mirroring exercise will introduce to you, as well as affirm, the wonderful person you are. Remember, you are what you think you are!

• • • Find a comfortable place to sit. Hold your love stone in your left hand and a mirror in your right hand. Or you may choose to stand in front of a vanity mirror to do this exercise.

• • • Look into the mirror and begin your deep breathing. Feel yourself becoming centered and relaxed.

• • • Now smile at yourself in the mirror and feel that you are inhaling a warm, loving, pink light. Continue doing this until you are comfortable looking at yourself.

• • • Once you are comfortable gazing at your reflection, repeat this affirmation out loud ten times as you rub your love stone: "I am a beautiful, loving, happy person."

• • • Now smile at yourself in the mirror and know that you are a beautiful, loving, happy person.

• • • Finish by repeating this affirmation out loud ten times as you rub your love stone: "I love you (*your full name*)."

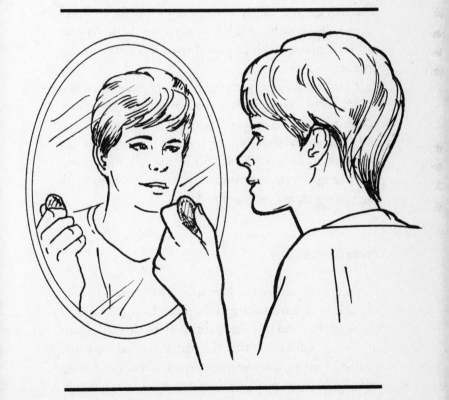

While you may feel silly or awkward at first, do this mirroring exercise daily. Make it a part of your grooming ritual; it's the perfect finishing touch and will instill self-love.

OVERCOMING SHYNESS

If you suffer from shyness, know that it can be corrected. The shyness you feel is a symptom of your lack of self-love, so work with the self-love exercises daily. As your self-love grows, much of your shyness will naturally disappear.

It's important to overcome shyness because when you are shy your energy is in a state of contraction. Since you're not sending any energy out it is difficult for you to begin new relationships or connect in a loving, open way with those around you. While the following photo exercise may seem extravagant, it is invaluable in helping you overcome your shyness.

Photo Exercise

If you are shy one of the best things you can do to help yourself is to have your picture taken by a professional photographer and then have it beautifully framed. Place it in your bedroom so that the first thing you see when you wake up in the morning is your attractive, loving self. Each night put your love stone in front of your picture before you go to bed and affirm, "I am charming and outgoing."

This exercise is constructive in many ways. The time and expense involved helps to reaffirm your self-worth. And going through the process of finding the right photographer, choosing your wardrobe, and being captured in your best light will help you realize what a special, lovable person you are. Shop around for a good photographer who will pamper you and make you feel as if you're a star; it'll do wonders for your self-esteem.

Carry your love stone with you to parties or any social gatherings. As you extend your right hand to introduce yourself, hold your love stone in your left hand and feel, believe, and see that you are charming and outgoing. Whenever self-doubt begins to emerge, focus on your love stone and know that it is beaming you full of self-love.

■   ■   ■

Remember that with the help of your love stone and the goodness of your heart you have the power to create an inner security nothing can destroy. All that is required is that you connect with and accept yourself—your true source of love.

WHEN MY FIRST MARRIAGE ENDED, I BEGAN LIVING A rather typical singles life-style: casual dates with men I had very little in common with and a few romances that quickly fizzled out. As career goals became my focus, I refused to recognize my need for a personal life. I was so intent on being independent and proving I could do it all on my own that I convinced myself love had no place in my life, at least not at that time.

One day I woke up in the country house I had rented

for the summer, isolated in the Green Mountains of Vermont, and realized that except for my cat, I was all alone. My family lived thousands of miles away, my friends were in Manhattan, and there I was—living alone on top of a mountain.

My writing career was flourishing and success felt good, but at what price? My heart ached with loneliness as I looked at the cozy chairs, the crackling fire, and the inviting kitchen that surrounded me. While my summer house was the perfect love nest, there was no one to share it with because I had barricaded my heart against love.

Looking back, I now realize it wasn't my career that kept me from finding love; it was my lack of emotional connection with myself. I had no understanding of what my personal needs were, the type of person I wanted to share my life with, or what I had to offer in a relationship. I had been so busy connecting with my mind that I had neglected my heart. I was out of touch with my emotional truths.

When I returned to Manhattan an enlightened friend began to tell me about all the good things he had been attracting into his life since he had started visualizing and affirming what he desired. He taught me the basics, which I immediately put to use. Within two months from the time I returned to Manhattan, I met my second husband. Had I known about crystals, specifically the power of the love stone, I might have attracted him into my life sooner!

FINDING LOVE

If you desire a quality love relationship, it takes action on your part. Simply wishing for a relationship is not going to bring love into your life. You must plan your "love" course of action with the same determination you would use if you were looking for a new job or a new place to live. However, finding love requires subtle action; you don't go knocking on doors begging to be loved.

The first and most important step to finding love is deciding that you really want it, you are ready for it, and you are worthy of it. This is why the previous chapter on self-love is so important and why you should continue to practice the self-love exercises as you send out your love energy.

When you feel worthy of love and truly desire it, your heart is open, ready to receive it. But not just from anyone; rather from the type of person *you choose* to attract into your life with the help of your love stone, visualizations, and affirmations. When used together, they create a powerful love magnet.

Visualizing Your Perfect Mate

• • • Lie down on a comfortable flat surface and bend your knees so that your lower back feels relaxed. Begin your deep breathing as you rub your love stone with your left hand. Continue for a few minutes, floating into a deep sense of relaxation.

• • • Once you begin to relax, inhale a loving pink light and as you exhale, affirm silently or out loud: "I am ready to receive and give love."

• • • Repeat this process seven times.

• • • Feel your emotional well-being and know that you are filled with love.

• • • Now place your love stone on the center of your chest and relax your arms at your side.

• • • As you continue your deep breathing, begin seriously visualizing the type of person you would like to attract into your life.

• • • First focus on your own needs and what you honestly think you can give to a relationship at this time in your life. What are your priorities? What characteristics do you think will best compliment your life-style?

• • • Now focus on the specific qualities you desire in a mate and begin to create this energy in your mind. For instance:

—What personality traits do you find the most appealing? (Sensitive, caring, introspective, tender, passionate, aggressive, outgoing, active . . .)

—How important is his/her professional status or income?

—Is it important that he/she wants to have a family, and if so to what extent do you want this to be the focus of your relationship?

—Do you need a lot of affection and attention or do you need someone who respects your need for privacy and space?

• • • Realizing that you can never get it all, out of all the qualities you desire in a mate, which one is the most important? This should always be your starting point whenever you visualize this person.

• • • Get a clear picture of this person, with as many details as possible, focusing on all the attributes that you desire. Be creative but also be realistic—focusing on the essence of the person rather than specific physical qualities.

• • • Now place your love stone on your third eye—between your brows and above your nose—and project your visualization into the stone. Stay with this visualization for a couple of minutes as you meet and get to know this person in your mind.

• • • Before you remove your love stone from your third eye, hold the visualization in your mind as you affirm out loud or silently: "So be it."

Until this person enters your life it is essential you do
this exercise from start to finish with the same visualization once a day. You should also continuously visualize
him/her several times a day: on your coffee break, during
lunch, while you're running errands, or walking the dog.
Simply hold your love stone in your right hand and see
this person clearly in your mind, replaying your original
visualization and projecting the energy out into the universe. The more time and energy you put into finding
love, the quicker your results.

Affirm your visualization by writing down a description of this person just as you have visualized—remember that the most important quality should come first.
Place your love stone on your written affirmation while
you sleep. Or put your stone and the written description
under your pillow, and you may just see this person in
your dreams!

REKINDLING THAT INITIAL SPARK

There's nothing more exciting about love than when it
is new. At the onset of that initial spark of love each
and every moment together is a thrill as you delight in
discovering all there is to know about each other. But
what about when the bloom has faded, when those initial thrills have become old hat? Whether in marriage or
in an ongoing relationship, to love someone "for better
or worse" is easier said than done.

If you find that you're bored with the present state of

your marriage or relationship, the following exercises may help rekindle that initial spark.

Passion Exercise

• • • Find a comfortable place to sit and hold your rose quartz to your heart. Begin your deep breathing.

• • • As you deep breathe, center yourself and clear your mind of any distracting thoughts.

• • • Remember how you felt and what it was like when you and your lover or spouse first met, how you felt when you fell in love. Remember every detail: Where did you go? What special things did you do together? What was it like when you first started making love?

• • • As you relive those early days, try to recall that special warmth of new love. Stay with these feelings as your memories unravel. Feel the love in your heart and realize how good it makes you feel. Know that your love stone is renewing that first blush of love.

• • • Stay with these feelings and gently affirm over and over again: "I am in love with (*spouse or lover's name*)."

Repeat this love exercise daily and take your love stone to bed with you at night. As you lie next to your lover or spouse, silently affirm "I am in love with you; I desire you" over and over. Don't be surprised if passion begins when your affirmation ends.

Mirroring Your Love

This exercise can remove apathy or indifference that has developed between you and your partner. However, in order for this to work, your partner must participate. As

you do this exercise together, your energies slowly merge, becoming one.

- • • Both of you should sit in a chair or on the floor, facing each other.

- • • Women, hold your love stone in your left hand. Men, hold your love stone in your right hand.

- • • As you face each other, close your eyes and begin your deep breathing. Center yourselves and clear your minds as you begin to relax.

- • • Now open your eyes and look into one another's eyes for at least five minutes; the longer you can do this, the more effective it is.

- • • As you look into one another's eyes, feel any emotional barriers begin to crumble. Each of you imagine that your heart is a lovely rose unfolding with love.

- • • Begin to send loving, tender thoughts to each other.

- • • Feel love and compassion for each other as you remember all the different experiences you have shared.

- • • Now simultaneously place your love stone against each other's heart.

- • • Holding this position, both of you affirm out loud: "Our love is renewed."

• • • Repeat this affirmation at least seven times, but
you may feel like continuing it for longer.

After this exercise hold each other, but remain silent for
five minutes. Now share what you feel and how you felt
during this exercise. Repeating this exercise once a week
will help you and your partner remain emotionally connected, regardless of how busy and independent you are.
This exercise also develops your intuition about each
other's needs.

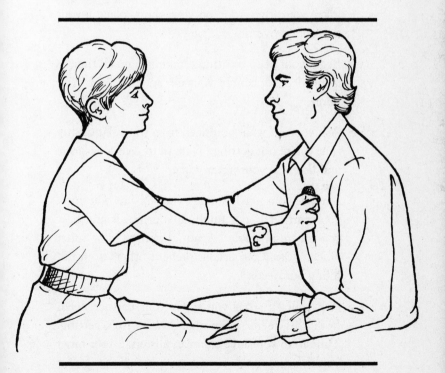

Creating Harmony Where There Is Chaos

If you and your partner have been arguing, both of you need to reconnect with the truth of your hearts. But let it begin with you. And let the soothing energy of your love stone help you dissolve the chaos and re-create the harmony in your relationship.

• • • Lie down on a comfortable flat surface with your knees bent so that your lower back is relaxed. Place your love stone on your chest, placing your right hand over it.

• • • Begin your deep breathing, taking as much time as is needed to center yourself and to clear your mind.

• • • Ask yourself what you need from this relationship that you're not getting. Tune in to your love stone and listen to your inner voice.

• • • Analyze your needs and ask yourself why you think your partner is not fulfilling your needs and how *you* are responsible. Again, listen to your inner voice. (Often *our actions* prevent others from fulfilling our needs.)

• • • Ask yourself what you think your partner needs from this relationship that he/she isn't getting. Tune in to your love stone and listen to your inner voice.

• • • Analyze your partner's needs and ask yourself why you think you are unable to fulfill them. Focus on one need in particular and ask yourself how you can fulfill it. Again, listen to your inner voice.

• • • Now visualize you and your partner together, communicating in a loving way. Hold this visualization for a few minutes.

After this exercise, as soon as possible do whatever is necessary to fulfill your partner's needs. This is a gesture of unconditional love. Repeat this exercise weekly. As you make an effort to fulfill your partner's needs, one by one you will find that your needs are being met too. The chaos will dissolve as your selfless actions fill your partner's heart with love. From your partner's heart, the love will return to you.

WHEN YOU THINK LOVE HAS ENDED

It can happen just like that. You wake up one morning, look at the person lying beside you, and realize that you feel nothing. You wonder what has happened, where love has gone. Or it can be a gradual process as each day you feel that the two of you are growing farther and farther apart. Perhaps your careers have taken you in different directions, your children are grown and gone, or you no longer share the same point of view about anything.

Regardless of how it happens, most relationships go through phases where either one or both of you are convinced that your love has ended. Before you start considering a trial separation or seeing a divorce lawyer, your love stone can help clarify your feelings and may bring to light some positive aspects of your relationship that you have overlooked, some positive aspects that make the relationship worth holding on to. What you think is the end of love may only be a transitional phase in your relationship that can pass in time if you make an effort to bring your love back to life.

Love Meditation

- • • Lie down on a comfortable flat surface with your knees bent so that your lower back is relaxed. With your love stone in your left hand, place your hand against your heart.

- • • Begin your deep breathing, allowing plenty of time to relax to center yourself and to clear your mind. Deeply inhale the loving pink light and exhale deeply any anxiety you may be feeling.

- • • Continue your deep breathing as you feel yourself going deeper and deeper within yourself. Imagine that you are on a journey to the center of your heart, where the truth lives.

• • • Now picture your partner in your mind. See him/
her exactly as he/she is in the present time, and as
you see him/her list everything that you don't like.

—Physical appearance

—Personal habits

—Attitude

—His/her friends

—How he/she spends free time

• • • Let all the bitterness, anger, and distaste that you
feel toward this person surface. Don't deny it. Stay
with it, feel its intensity, and then feel your heart
release it as you exhale deeply. You may want to
blow out as you exhale.

• • • Continue inhaling pink light and exhaling your
negative emotions until you feel that they are
completely released.

• • • Now relax with some gentle deep breathing for
about one minute.

• • • Again, picture your partner in your mind as he/
she is in the present time. Now focus on the qualities that still appeal to you. Remember the times
you have shared, good and bad, and how this person has provided you with emotional support.
Reenact these memories in your mind as vividly as
possible and stay with them for a while.

• • • Now relax with some gentle deep breathing for about one minute.

• • • This time picture yourself alone in your home. Walk through each room and look into each closet, noticing that the only things that exist are your own. See yourself living alone. Think of how you would feel waking up alone in the morning and going to bed alone at night. Take yourself through your daily routine, knowing that your partner is no longer a part of your life. Try to imagine how it will feel to have someone who was once so familiar to you removed from your life. Elaborate on this visualization as much as possible. The further you take it, the more clarity you'll gain.

• • • Now ask yourself, "How will I feel if this person is no longer a part of my life?" Make yourself see, believe, and feel that the relationship is over. *How do you feel?*

• • • Let your emotions emerge freely. Don't deny anything that you feel. Don't be surprised if you start crying. Stay with it, experience it, flow with it.

• • • Rest for five minutes before you get up. I think that you will be amazed by the new insights you have gained. Wait two days before repeating this meditation so that you can continue to process and release the emotions you experienced.

After you have done this meditation a couple of times you may decide your relationship is worth fighting for, is worth nurturing back to life. If this is the case, repeat on a regular basis the Passion exercise, Mirroring Your Love, and Creating Harmony Where There Is Chaos.

THE RELATIONSHIPS YOU HAVE HAD WITH YOUR FAMILY, especially since childhood, affect all your adult relationships. For it is your earliest childhood experiences, the degree of love, affection, and parental approval you received that create the basis of your self-love.

LOVING MOM AND DAD UNCONDITIONALLY

While you love your parents, you probably experience moments when you think to yourself, "If only Mom and Dad had done this for me." Or, "If only they hadn't made me do that, things might be different for me now." You must accept that the past is the past and that it can't be changed. It's important to realize that whatever mistakes you feel your parents made in raising you, chances are good that they did the best they could given their own circumstances. Remember that they were also once children and might have been deprived of the love and understanding that would have made them better parents.

Although you have no power to erase the past, you do have the power to harmonize your present and future relationships with your parents. In the following exercises you will be working on forgiving your parents and then sending them unconditional love. Working with these exercises will help ease any anger, emotional pain, or accumulated bitterness that is lodged in your heart.

Forgiveness

• • • Lie down on a comfortable flat surface with your knees bent so that your lower back is relaxed. Place your love stone on your chest.

• • • Begin your deep breathing and relax as you inhale a loving pink light and exhale any anxiety or tension you may be feeling. Feel yourself becoming centered as your mind clears.

• • • Now begin to list in your mind any painful childhood experiences that you remember, for instance:

—Did one or both of your parents have a drinking problem?

—Did their professional life/lives deprive you of the attention you needed?

—Did they give you enough affection?

—Were you punished when you didn't deserve it?

—Do you feel that they loved your brothers/sisters more than they loved you?

—Did your accomplishments go unnoticed?

• • • Let every painful experience that wants to emerge surface. Now inhale deeply the loving pink light and exhale deeply these memories. If you begin to cry, go with it; just let it all out and release it into the past where it belongs.

• • • Now begin chanting this affirmation over and over again: "I forgive you Mom/Dad for all the hurts, both real and imagined."

• • • Rest for about five minutes before you get up.

• • • You need time to accept what you have just honestly confronted, so don't repeat this exercise more often than every two days. However, do continue this exercise on a regular basis. The more time you spend with it, the better your relationship with your parents will become.

Sending Unconditional Love

After you have completed the forgiveness exercise, you'll want to send your parents unconditional love.

• • • Sit up and with your love stone in your right hand, hold it against your heart. Continue with your deep breathing.

• • • Now visualize your parents' faces smiling at you. Enclose them in a clear pink bubble.

• • • Imagine that you are beaming from your heart through your love stone and into their bubble a beautiful pink ray of light. Affirm while you do this: "I love you Mom and Dad, no matter what."

• • • Continue visualizing and affirming, knowing that you are sending them your love, unconditionally. Send your unconditional love to your parents every day. Make it a part of your daily routine.

If one or both of your parents are deceased, it is still important that you do these exercises. You need to for-

give them and release any negative feelings you still hold in your heart. These are the feelings that prevent you from loving and letting love into your heart.

You can also repeat both of these exercises for any relative you are having a conflict with, whether it concerns something from the past or something that is happening at the present time. Before a family reunion send unconditional love to each family member who will be attending. Keep your love stone with you during the reunion. You may have to rub it from time to time to remind yourself that you love them *all* unconditionally —even your cousin Margaret, who stole your first boyfriend when you were both sixteen!

YOUR CHILDREN

If you are a parent yourself, it may be easier for you to understand and forgive your parents' mistakes. I know that once I started having children, I became less critical of my own upbringing. I began to have a better understanding of the difficulties my parents must have faced. Personally, I find parenting one of the most challenging jobs I've ever had. But those sweet kisses and hugs I receive compensate for all the demands of parenting.

My children are both under the age of five. Although I scold and punish them when necessary, I also show how much I love them. I make it a point to tell them several times a day that I love them. When I'm away on business, I talk to them first thing in the morning and before they go to bed at night, telling them about my day and that I love them.

I also use my love stone to send love to them from wherever I am. I simply hold my love stone in my right hand, visualize my children in my mind, and send them lots and lots of love. I also put my love stone on their pictures at night; it gives me peace of mind, even though I won't be available if they cry out in the middle of the night. Grandparents can also do this to feel closer to their grandchildren if they don't have the opportunity to see them often. Use your crystal to keep connections strong when you have to live on long-distance love.

I've given each of my children a love stone to use while I'm away—ones large enough so that there is no danger of their swallowing them. This way they feel that part of me is still with them, no matter where I am. My

three-year-old daughter calls her love stone her "magic rock." She is convinced that the love it holds for her protects her from the monsters that live in the closet. Even when I'm home, she refuses to go to bed unless her love stone is on the windowsill at night.

While the magic rock theory seems to work wonders on my young children, I suspect that the effect won't be as powerful when they become teenagers. If you continue to work with your love stone, filling your heart and home with love and teach your children about the power of visualization, affirmation, and the love stone, I believe these emotional tools can make adolescence easier and provide a smoother transition into adulthood.

MAINTAINING FRIENDSHIPS

Whether you're single, living with someone, or married, friendships are an important part of your emotional well-being. Friends can provide you with love and support when the rest of the world, including your own family, seems to be letting you down. Good friends are the people you can count on no matter what and, therefore, deserve lots of love from you in return. Nurture them as you would nurture your own family members, and try to do something special for each one of them at least once a week, even if it is only picking up the phone and saying, "Hi! How are you? Do you need anything?"

Try the following exercise to enhance your existing friendships and to attract new friends into your life.

Taking Care of Your Friends

• • • Find a comfortable place to sit and hold your love stone in your right hand. Begin your deep breathing.

• • • Visualize each of your friends. See them standing in a line together holding hands.

• • • Now see yourself going down the line giving each friend a big hug. Tell your friends how much they mean to you and how much you appreciate each one of them. Thank them for being in your life.

• • • Rub your love stone and imagine that it is sending loving energy to each of them, filling their hearts with your love.

• • • Now affirm, silently or out loud: "I surround myself with loving and supportive people."

• • • Continue this affirmation as you inhale loving pink light and exhale the affirmation.

This is also an excellent affirmation to work with when you have moved to a new home or changed jobs. Simply rub your love stone in your right hand and repeat the affirmation several times a day until you meet new friends and feel comfortable in your new environment.

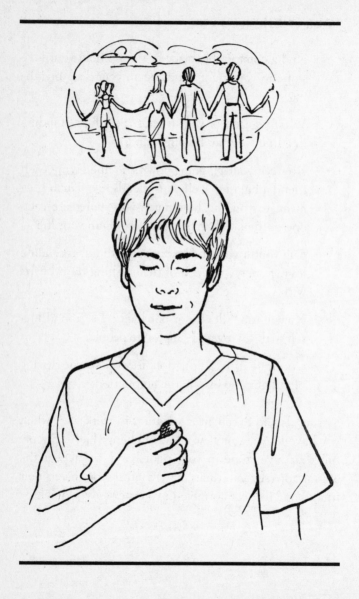

WHEN FRIENDS BECOME RIVALS

You've received a promotion, come into an inheritance, bought a new house, or had a baby. And of course you want to share all of your good news with your friends. While most of your friends will be thrilled to hear of your good fortune, there may be a few who become envious. You know when this happens because you can feel a subtle shift in their attitude toward you. They may suddenly become cynical or critical of your life. You may learn that they are saying unkind things about you behind your back.

Their envy, you hope, will quickly pass. You can facilitate this by shifting the attention to them. While you may be chomping at the bit eager to fill them in on the latest bit of news, focus on what is going on in their lives instead. Compliment them, praise them—say whatever you can to make them feel good, to make them feel secure about the direction their life is taking.

You can also use your love stone to ease the envy.

• • • Simply hold your love stone in your right hand, imagine you and your friend warmly embracing, and send your friend unconditional love. Affirm out loud or silently, "I love you _____ no matter what." Repeat this easy exercise before and after you spend time with your envious friend.

However, a little bit of envy can be healthy; it sharpens your competitive edge, motivating you to achieve your own goals. If you're feeling envious of another person, let that person serve as a role model, reminding you that you too can have and be what you want to be if you focus your energy on your special talents and attributes. Don't throw focus by wasting your precious time and energy envying what someone else has or is doing. Instead, get to work on yourself. If you find this difficult to do, concentrate on the self-love exercises. This will help you keep your focus on yourself as you develop and improve your own abilities.

JEALOUSY: YOURS AND THEIRS

While envy can be constructive, fueling your competitive spirit, jealousy is a negative emotion that is ultimately self-destructive because it makes you act out in negative ways. Envy, the desire to possess what others have, is an emotion that can be channeled very positively. Your envy of your friends's great new job, for example, doesn't have to mean that you wish her career *wasn't* blossoming, but rather that you would like to have an equally nice job as well. Which in turn might inspire you to go out and do just that. Jealousy, on the other hand, is sexual and often secretive in nature. Since it stems from an unhealthy insecurity or need to control others, it can bring great unhappiness both to you and the other people in your life. Depending on the degree of jealousy you feel toward another, you may become manipulative, devious, bitter, and even nasty. If your jealousy grows and you lose emotional control, your negative actions only attract more negativity into your life as you block your love flow. If you allow jealousy to control your emotions you could end up alone and miserable—the signals you're sending out are anything but warm and loving.

Jealousy stems from feelings of lack, the fear that "there isn't enough for me," as well as any feelings of inadequacy you carry within yourself. Perhaps you feel physically inadequate, that you're not attractive enough to keep your mate interested in only you.

So afraid of losing the one you love, you may feel anxious everytime your mate talks to another member of the opposite sex or does anything that deviates from the normal routine. As you become suspicious and possessive, your jealousy can eventually repel the very person you're trying to keep.

Whatever its cause, if you feel that jealousy is one of your emotional stumbling blocks I urge you to take the time to work it out. Again, you need to go back and work with the self-love exercises, indulging yourself in your own wonderful uniqueness. This will help you develop your inner security so that you believe in your ability to love and be lovable. Also, your weekly *emotional tune-up* (refer to Chapter 3) is the perfect time to work on releasing your jealousy.

On a daily basis there are two affirmations that you should use with your love stone:

• • • First, to help you remove your fear of being deprived:

—Center yourself with some deep breathing.

—Rub your love stone in your *left hand* (receiving), and on each inhale imagine that you are filling up with a rich pink light.

—On each exhale, affirm silently or out loud: "My life is filled with abundance."

—And then: "I am secure within myself."

• • • This second affirmation may be difficult at first. It requires that you send unconditional love to the person who is the focus of your jealousy:

—Center yourself with some deep breathing.

—Rub your love stone in your *right hand* (sending), and on each inhale imagine you are filling up with a rich pink light.

—On each exhale, affirm silently or out loud: "I am happy for you (*whomever you are jealous of*)."

With these two affirmations you are at once soothing your emotions and repairing your relationship with the other person. Keep your love stone with you at all times and repeat these affirmations several times a day.

If you feel that you are the victim of someone else's jealousy, try the same tactics you would use to diffuse envy. Tell them that they're terrific, ask them what's going on in their life—try to make them feel special. Overwhelm them with kindness.

If this doesn't work and their hostility becomes worse you may have to distance yourself from them for a while. This is for your sake because jealousy can destroy your well-being, making you feel guilty for being happy when they're not. As I said earlier, guilt is a form of self-punishment that nobody deserves.

Letting Go

• • • Center yourself, breathing deeply. Hold your love stone in your *right hand.*

• • • While rubbing your love stone, inhale a warm pink light.

• • • See the jealous person in your mind. Enclose them in a pink bubble and watch them float away.

• • • Now affirm silently or out loud: "I release you (*friend's name*) with love. I forgive you for all hurts, both real and imagined."

• • • Know, feel, and see that you have released this person and the negativity around them from your life.

You may also want to write the affirmation out and place your love stone on this affirmation for twenty-four hours. Again, in your mind, wish them well and release them from your energy field until they are ready to love again.

I find this simple process very powerful because you are releasing them from your life with love, not hostility. If they are true friends, they will reenter your life when they are ready.

AS YOUR HEART HOLDS MANY SECRETS, YOUR LOVE STONE
has many uses. One of the reasons it is so effective in
soothing emotional conflicts is because it is so easy to
use. Just carrying the stone with you, allowing its soothing energy to merge with your energy, will make you feel
better. Holding it in your hand from time to time and
looking at it will remind you that all of life is full of love,
waiting for you to open up your heart and receive it. No
one has to suffer from a lack of love in their life.

While the preceding love exercises are very important for developing and enhancing your emotional well-being, there are also lots of quick techniques that you can use to ease those little conflicts. In most cases these involve nothing more than holding your love stone and affirming "what is." You can elaborate on these basics according to your needs. Here are a few of my love stone favorites that alleviate some of my daily emotional conflicts:

RELEASING YOUR ANGER

When someone says or does something that makes you angry, you don't have to let it ruin your day. Instead, hold your love stone in your right hand and begin your deep breathing to calm yourself. Now imagine that your anger is moving out of your heart through your right shoulder, down your right arm, and into your stone. Let your love stone absorb all of your negative emotions. As you clean and clear your stone under running tap water, affirm: "I release my anger."

Keep repeating the affirmation as the water runs over your stone, until you feel completely purged.

YOU DESERVE PROSPERITY

Your relationship with prosperity is similar to your relationship with yourself. If you don't love and accept your-

self, it is difficult for you to attract love into your life; if
you don't feel that you deserve to be prosperous, then it
is difficult to attract prosperity into your life.

Several times a day with your love stone in your right
hand, visualize yourself doing the kind of work you like
and being very successful as you do it. Hold your stone
to your third eye—above your nose and between your
brows—and program your prosperity into it. See success,
feel success, and believe that success is yours.

Now remove your stone from your third eye and just
hold it in your right hand as you affirm: "I am prosperous." Repeat several times.

I use this affirmation all the time. Whenever I'm pre-
paring for an important meeting or starting a new project, I take a few minutes out of every hour and affirm
that I deserve prosperity. I repeat this to myself over and
over, whether I'm walking to my appointment or driv-
ing. When I was applying for a bank loan and credit
cards, I affirmed that "I deserve prosperity" for one minute every waking hour.

CREATING YOUR SELF-IMAGE

Regardless of how terrific we really look, few of us are
ever pleased with our bodies because we demand perfec-
tion. As your self-love develops you will be more realistic, accepting yourself as you are at the moment. But if
you do need to lose or gain a few pounds, let your love
stone help you create the figure you desire.

• • • Find a comfortable place to sit and hold your love stone in your left hand. Begin your deep breathing to center yourself and clear your mind.

• • • Imagine that you are sitting on the beach, *watching yourself* swimming and frolicking in the ocean. Hold this visualization for a few moments.

• • • Now see yourself emerging from the surf, looking radiant, beautiful, and sun-kissed. See your body as you would like it to be walking toward you as you sit on the beach. Allow yourself to walk toward you until your old body and new body have merged into one. Imagine that the transformation is already taking place.

• • • By repeating this visualization often and using your love stone as a reminder that you have the power to create what you want, you will be inspired to change your diet and exercise habits to create the figure you desire.

DEPROGRAMMING YOUR NEGATIVE SELF-JUDGMENTS

Remember, you are what you think you are. Turn any negatives you feel about yourself into positives with this simple exercise:

With your love stone placed at the top of your paper,

on the left side list every negative emotion you feel about yourself. For instance:

—Nothing good ever happens to me

—Nobody loves me

—I am an unattractive person

Now on the right side of the paper turn each negative into a positive affirmation. For instance:

—The universe provides me with everything I need

—I am loved by everyone

—I am a beautiful person

Now hold your love stone in your left hand and affirm your positive affirmations. Keep your list with you and repeat it several times a day. You can also wrap your list around your love stone and keep it in your pocket.

YOUR GRATITUDE LIST

At the end of each day sit at a table or desk with your love stone placed at the top of a piece of paper. Begin to list everything that happened during the day for which you are grateful. For instance:

—Did you have lunch out with friends?

—Did your boss compliment you?

—Was your energy high?

—Did you have a pleasant phone conversation with a relative?

—Did you have fun with your children?

—Did you notice how beautiful the trees look or appreciate the design of a new building that's going up?

This list should contain everything you can think of that made you happy or brought a smile to your face. Making your gratitude list is especially helpful when you feel like you've had a bad day, as it reminds you how much you have in your life for which to be grateful.

As you read your list, hold your love stone in your left hand. Let your gratitude fill your heart as you focus on the beauty and joy of life.

CONCLUSION

WHILE YOUR ROSE QUARTZ CRYSTAL IS AN INVALUABLE tool to help you fill your life with love, there are no shortcuts or easy answers when it comes to sustaining love. All relationships, from friends to lovers, demand constant nurturing and understanding if they are to be happy and fulfilling. Practice the love exercises regularly and give all of your relationships the love and attention they deserve.

As you develop your ability to love unconditionally,

you will become a flowing channel of love, attracting more love into your life than you could have ever imagined. You will learn the truth of your heart and whenever you connect with it you will be renewed. For the love you learn to show yourself and others will provide you with an infinite abundance of joy and harmony in your life.

As you visualize and affirm, seeing, believing, and feeling your ability to love, know that the magic energy of your love stone combined with the goodness of your heart will fill your life with love. Where there is love there are no endings—only beginnings. This is the magic of love.

ABOUT THE AUTHOR

CONNIE CHURCH is a free-lance writer. She is the coauthor of *Self-Massage, Powercise: The Elaine Powers Total Workout Guide,* and *Starstyle: An Astrological Guide to Love and Beauty.* Her first book, *Self-Massage,* has been published in nine different languages and is currently in print throughout the world.

In addition, Connie has ghostwritten several celebrity books, including Marisa Berenson's *Dressing Up.* Her articles, covering a wide range of interests including health, beauty, fashion, psychology, and metaphysics, have appeared in national magazines and newspapers across the country. Connie's most recent book is *Crystal Clear: How to Use the Earth's Magic Energy to Vitalize Your Body, Mind, and Spirit.*